Insect World

Dragonflies

by Mari Schuh

Bullfrog
Books

Ideas for Parents and Teachers

Bullfrog Books let children practice reading informational text at the earliest reading levels. Repetition, familiar words, and photo labels support early readers.

Before Reading

- Discuss the cover photo. What does it tell them?

- Look at the picture glossary together. Read and discuss the words.

Read the Book

- "Walk" through the book and look at the photos.
- Let the child ask questions. Point out the photo labels.

- Read the book to the child, or have him or her read independently.

After Reading

- Prompt the child to think more. Ask: Have you ever seen a dragonfly? Were there other dragonflies nearby? What color were they?

The author dedicates this book to Avery and Cami Schuh.

Bullfrog Books are published by Jump!
5357 Penn Avenue South
Minneapolis, MN 55419
www.jumplibrary.com

Library of Congress Cataloging-in-Publication Data

Schuh, Mari C., 1975- author.
  Dragonflies / by Mari Schuh.
    pages cm -- (Insect world) (Bullfrog books)
  Audience: 5-8.
  Audience: K to grade 3.
  Summary: "This photo-illustrated book for early readers tells how dragonflies fly and hunt for food. Includes picture glossary."-- Provided by publisher.
  Includes bibliographical references and index.
  ISBN 978-1-62031-083-0 (hardcover) --
ISBN 978-1-62496-151-9 (ebook)
  1. Dragonflies--Juvenile literature. I. Title.
II. Series: Schuh, Mari C., 1975- Insect world.
  QL520.S38 2015
  595.7'33--dc23

                              2013037887

Series Editor: Rebecca Glaser
Series Designer: Ellen Huber
Book Designer: Anna Peterson
Photo Researcher: Kurtis Kinneman

All photos by Shutterstock except: Danita Delimont/ Alamy, 14–15; iStock, 3b, 4, 8–9, 23tl; Mat Smith, 12–13, 23bl; Michael Durham/Minden Pictures/ Corbis, 15; Stephen Dalton/Nature Picture Library, 10; Tony Ashton, 18–19

Printed in the United States of America at Corporate Graphics, in North Mankato, Minnesota.
6-2014
10 9 8 7 6 5 4 3 2 1

Table of Contents

Fast Dragonflies

A dragonfly rests.

The hot sun warms its wings.

Now it can fly.

6

It can look for bugs to eat.

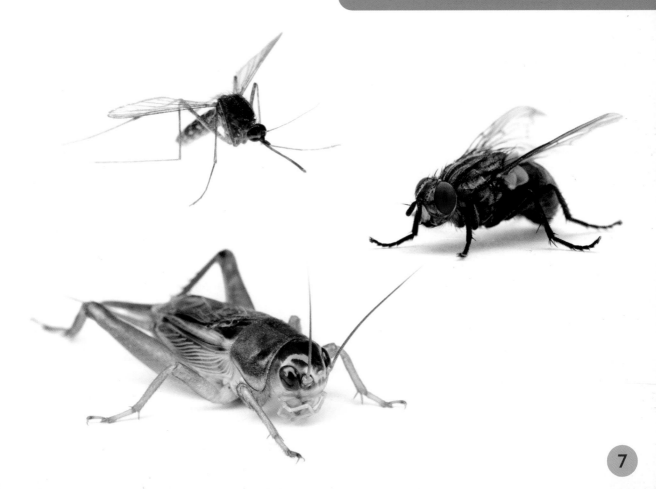

7

The dragonfly has four clear wings.

It flies up and down.

It hovers in the sky.

wing

Zoom! Zoom!

It can fly as fast as a car in town.

The dragonfly
hunts for food.

It flies to a pond.

Huge eyes let it
see **all** around.

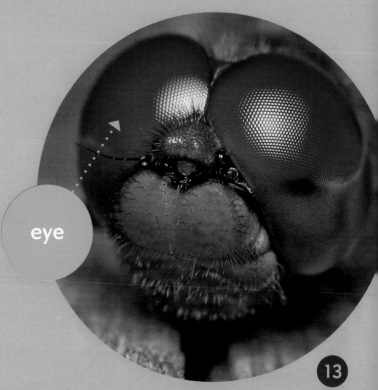

eye

13

Look out!

A bullfrog jumps out.

14

The dragonfly
flies away.

15

See the bee?

The dragonfly grabs
its prey in the air.

Munch! Munch!

The dragonfly eats it up.
It eats as it flies.

The dragonfly sits in the sun.

It rests.

Then it will hunt again.

Parts of a Dragonfly

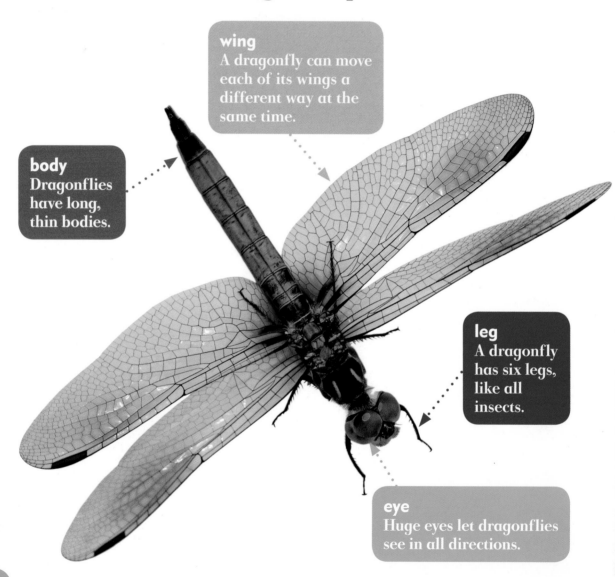

wing
A dragonfly can move each of its wings a different way at the same time.

body
Dragonflies have long, thin bodies.

leg
A dragonfly has six legs, like all insects.

eye
Huge eyes let dragonflies see in all directions.

Picture Glossary

hover
To stay in one
place in the air.

pond
A small body
of water.

hunt
To look for
insects and
animals to eat.

prey
Insects and
animals that
are hunted
for food.

Index

To Learn More

Learning more is as easy as 1, 2, 3.

1) Go to www.factsurfer.com

2) Enter "dragonflies" into the search box.

3) Click the "Surf" button to see a list of websites.

With factsurfer.com, finding more information is just a click away.